The System for Her,
Part 1
Doc Love Lessons in Betty Neels Books

Janice Seto

DEDICATION

Thomas Hodges, www.DocLove.com

and

The Ladies of The Uncrushable Jersey Dress
http://everyneelsthing.blogspot.com/
who appreciate the pairing of The System's Gentleman with Betty Neel's
old-fashioned girl

It never goes out of style!

CONTENTS

JANICE SETO

PREFACE

The moment I bought my own copy of *The Dating Dictionary/The System* by Doc Love (www.doclove.com) , I knew it was my best non-fiction book purchase ever. The System is based on over 10,000 interviews with women by Doc Love and written to help men with relationships. But it offers universal truths for women too!

It also is funny and it is insightful. It even has a diagram! (The Truth Triangle). As I kept reading it (the requisite minimum 15 times), the life lessons came alive. Of all the types of men in the world, Doc Love advises his disciples to become a 'Gentleman' or 'GentleMan' by emulating the best of the Cary Grant movies.

I think of Roger O Thornhill in Alfred Hitchcock's North by Northwest. He's witty, clever, proactive, and later on, is kindness itself. Looking for Miss Right to bring home to Mom, he leads with his heart, not his hormones. On the screen is the Gentleman personified.

I suddenly realized Doc Love's Gentleman is in print too. Women tend to be book readers – romance novels of every way to get to Happily Ever After (HEA) are our gender's guilty pleasure! Here he is, the hero of every Betty Neels novel!

For those of you who never heard of the British author, she was a retired nurse who published her first book at the age of 59 and wrote a total of 135 stories before her passing. Harlequin Mills & Boon still reprint her books which the author firmly kept free of pre-marital relations AKA 'going to Brighton' as the fansite

The Uncrushable Jersey Dress would put it (www.everyneelsthing.blogspot.com). Instead, Mrs Neels (the pseudonym of Evelyn Jessy Meier) filled her books with many a rich Dutch or British doctor/physician/surgeon (RDD and RBD) and the rare outlier other professional who are all GentleMen in the Doc Love sense of the term. In this book, I take pleasure in pointing out exactly how the men of Doc Love's *The System* show up in Betty Neels's books, from the Wimpus Americanus to Macho Boy to the top prize, the 3%er Gentleman.

And Betty Neels and Doc Love are on the same page as well on how we ladies can do to make the best of ourselves for our own sake. And his rule "One Chance Per Girl Per Lifetime" swings both ways – Alethea should have read The Dating Dictionary to recover from Dr Brighton Boy! (But then we would not have the book '*Sun and Candlelight*' - although that would have spared Alethea from the horrid twins…)

It has taken years of reflecting and research myself to adapt The System in its men-focused form to this 4-part book series, *The System for Women*:

1. Overview

2. Hero

3. Heroine

4. Happily Ever After Ladies, here are the collectively nuggets of the HEA from Betty Neels and Doc Love…

Ladies, let's see what we have…

ACKNOWLEDGMENTS

I came across Thomas Hodges's regular hilarious columns 'Doc Love' about 15 years ago and it has changed my life. For one, I am seeing humorous moments every day – with great pleasure and gratitude.

His book, *The Dating Dictionary*, is aimed at men. When I asked when The Dating Dictionary for Women would be published, he said to take *The Dating Dictionary* and just reverse it. Or write it myself.

After 15 years of taking his advice, why stop now?

This one's for you, Doc! *The System for Women*

To Thomas Hodges
And your sidekick, Jeff Stevens

1. Want a HEA? First, Do the Prep Work To Pass the Test

What is the test, ladies? It is The Physical Attraction Test.

That is the easy first step to get to a Happily Ever After (HEA) with a decent Gentleman – as Doc Love says, the Gentleman will pursue you only if you attract him ie 'pass the physical attraction test'. Men only bestir themselves for someone to whom he is attracted and finds appealing. It is called Interest Level (IR).

It is the same thing applies to us, ladies. Interest Level is like a thermometer with 100 degrees. At 50% Interest Level, you want to get to know the other person better ie go out on a date. Below that, you do not.

When a man does not pass our physical attraction test, we do not even entertain the idea of being HEA with him. You cannot explain why you don't feel chemistry with someone – the feeling is simply non-existent. And no matter how much your Aunt Mary or Mom or Grandfather think he is great and give you reasons why he is marriage material, you just do not feel anything. Being a lady, you do not waste his time or your time or his money going on a date with someone you have less than 50% IR in.

(Now, some people with not the slightest interest will go out on a date. Why? For other reasons, like career advancement (the odious Tom in *Wedding Bells for Beatrice*), reflected glory (Melville likes her as quality arm candy in *Off With the Old Love*), maybe did not want to stay in that night, wanted to try out a new restaurant or feeling lonely. Of course, women also do make exceptions for someone with the keys to a huge bank account - and that means she is not a lady! Looking at you, Helen van Trompe of *Discovering Daisy*). Does it make him or her a bad person? No, but it does not do them any favours either! A mutual attraction is the vital first element to a chance at a HEA.

His Best Self Made Easy

Here is how it looks when Ladies and Gentlemen put their best self forward. The heroes in Betty Neels's book are always depicted as well-groomed. Mrs Neels goes into detail as to how he is appropriately dressed in public – his suits (at his place of work and at expensive restaurants), his morning coat (at weddings), his black tie (at the ball), his white tails (formal reception). This means the Gentleman is an adult who won't embarrass you in public. He is a grown up! Someone you can take home to Mother.

In private, he is found in his splendid dressing gown (not a bathrobe), his slacks (never jeans), his hat (never baseball caps), his hair professionally short (no man-bun). This is not someone you have to mother to get out of his sweat pants and raggedy T-shirt swearing undying allegiance to some football team…

The only thing we women can do to pass someone's physical attraction test is to put our best foot forward. Every day. Put it out there. What is 'it'? Your best self.

Note this has nothing to do with fashion.

When a man doesn't pass our physical attraction test, there is a smart way to turn down his offer of a date. We women are wise not to bluntly say that truth, and give him the unvarnished answer of rejection "You don't attract me." Enough men don't handle rejection well that Doc Love advises we give him a bone for his ego, "I have a boyfriend…" Because men can deal with not trespassing on another man's preserves. But stark rejection? Not so much.

Her Best Self Made Easy
Similarly, in Betty Neels, the heroine dresses like a lady, not exposing her charms to all and sundry nor providing free advertising to some fashion house ('At least the girl did not wear a skirt up to her thighs and one of those vulgar tops printed with some stupid sentence.' *The Fortunes of Francesca*, by Betty Neels).

A lady wears what makes her look her best. Only you can figure out your best self. Sadly, it is only by trial-and-error (very few of us can look through our high school photos without cringing) and taking advice from someone impartial with a good eye can you avoid what doesn't work with you. Like the heroine in *Discovering Daisy* with that striking (not in a good way!) red dress.

How to pass the Physical Attraction Test: five easy steps. The five senses, as many a Betty Neels novel has the heroine indulging in:

1. <u>Smell</u> – a long bath and then a splash of Dioressence (or something else of quality). But it must suit your personality or your Walle will point out the disconnect to his Philomena of that expensive re-gift of Vu… (*Philomena's Miracle*)

2. <u>Taste</u> – no cigarette, gum, nor recreational drugs on the breath (so not fitting for the RDD's swoop)

3. <u>Touch</u> – texture – neat, non-greasy hair and buffed nails, the antithesis of the garish talons of The Veronica, our heroine's nemesis (known in *The System* as a Blocker).

4. <u>Hear</u> – No clickety-clack of skyhigh heels, no grating-on-the-ears bray (that belongs to the rescue donkey in the stable) and definitely ladylike vocabulary. Although the rare beastly Dutch oaths are well deployed…

5. <u>See</u> – Smile! Natural, not that 'show the Hollywood teeth of Kate Middleton' to all and sundry. Rather, a lady smiles with her eyes. And all Betty Neels heroines have lovely eyes.

From your front door, go into the world by giving it your best shot.

If a man is not interested in your best self, then that's it. It is failure to launch, not rejection. It is lack of chemistry, clear and simple. That's all there is to it. As Doc says, Believe it now.

The worst reaction to his indifference is to be hard on yourself. It is not a reflection on you. In *The Girl with Green Eyes*, Lucy Lockitt keeps putting a trip on herself: "I am not clever" and "I am plain." And it just gets tired! It has nothing to do with you. Just as you are not required to explain why you are not attracted to every Gentleman who walks past.

Don't give him another thought. Don't think it is a reflection on him and his intelligence. Speculating that he is stupid does you no credit.

Don't waste your time and energy on someone who has actually saved you time by expressing that you are not his type.

Do not put any more emotion into him. Don't feel bad or glad – be accepting of the reality and be indifferent too. It is what it is. Never develop a taste for bitter sandwiches. After all, it is not the end of the world.

Your ideal response should be a four-letter word. Unlike other women without Doc Love's The System - who put more money and time and effort to attract him - you can mentally check him off your list and say, "Next!"

After all, there are other fish in the sea. The very attractive head operating room nurse Deborah Culpeper starts the book, *Stars Through The Mist*, reflecting on dating widely over the previous two years.

Women who can't get past his indifference are wasting their time. Do not chase after someone who is running away from you.

And for heaven's sake, don't act as a Blocker of the woman he does show an interest in. Betty Neels portrays how pathetic it is – and for what? In *The Innocent Bride*, Dr Maureen Soames, 29, had her medical degree, training to specialize in haemotology, was heiress to her aunt, Lady Truscott, and her Manor house in a village in the West Country. Maureen had good looks and the guile to set her cap at wealthy consultant, Professor Simon Glenville, 39. As a newcomer to his haematology team, she was conveniently omnipresent every day to show off her looks and her brains.

He was not interested.

Maureen's reaction to his disinterest was to pour more effort into that lost cause. She asked him for lifts to The Manor as it was on his way (wanting to show off what real estate she would be getting). And on one Sunday night, she had the audacity to call him at his country house with the outlandish request to drive all the way to The Manor to fetch her and then to transport her to London – a bait he turned down with a terse 'Get a taxi'. For months, she kept hatching up every scheme possible to demonstrate what a good pair they would make – and how well matched they were.

Well, that was her opinion. He never shared it.

When all THAT did not result in his asking her out on a date, Maureen grasps at straws with a jumping-to-conclusion world record. Professor Glenville gives her lifts to the village therefore she, Dr Maureen Soames, must have a beach head!

Really, we all shake our heads when a brainy woman throws herself at a man who doesn't care that she are available – "…You would have been a fool if you had gone on with it and tried to alter something which couldn't be altered…" Mrs Potts to her daughter, Serena in *An Uncertain Summer.*

Rather, that is her variation of desperation.

Certainly it was Maureen's version of fake-it-til-you-make it, telling her aunt and everyone within shouting distance that Professor Glenville was about to propose. (How a woman can fool herself into believing a man who has never asked you out is on the cusp of popping the question… Self-deception, indeed.)

Maureen even took the risky step of taking that tale to the ears of any single woman in the village. In warning off prospective rivals, Maureen was being a Blocker to potential rivals such as bucolic beauty, Katrina Gibbs, 24.

Unfortunately, Simon Glenville was already 3 months into his courtship of Katrina by the time Maureen came into the picture. All her efforts were for naught…

This is what it is like when someone passes the Physical Attraction test as Katrina does Simon's. Despite Katrina living off the beaten path - and doing nothing to encourage him – she basically has to beat him off with a stick! Simon comes up with the most outlandish excuses to be in the neighbourhood to see the crisp and correct Miss Gibbs.

The Professor simply HAS to meet her personally at her home, Rose Cottage, about Aunt Thirza's diagnosis, then he returns a couple weeks later with a moss rose bush for transplanting and to tell her about Aunt Thirza's failing rapidly. Three weeks later, he drives down the morning after his European lecture tour to express his condolences.

With Katrina grieving her aunt's passing, Simon wisely kept his rising Interest Level under wraps, disguising his visits as 'passing by'. Maureen's aunt living in Katrina's village was a God-send to the professor – he had the excuse of giving Maureen lifts to Lady Truscott to order to drop in to see the object of his affections. If you read closely, he first agrees to give Maureen a lift to her aunt's… in order to be Johnny-on-the-spot to see Katrina. Anxious to get to Rose Cottage, he declines tea at the Manor – this Gentleman does not in any way lead Maureen on. Unlike other heroes in the Betty Neels novels, Simon focuses his tea drinking time on who counts. And this is all before he inveigles to house juvenile leukemia patient Tracy Ward and her mother at Katrina's for a summer respite. Oh, the many opportunities afforded Simon to travel down to see his little patient…

The boy is underfoot – Katrina can't turn around without tripping over Simon and his great socking Bentley.

Even if Simon had not met Katrina, it would not matter. When it comes to Maureen Soames, he is simply not interested.

Maureen's machinations were ultimately pointless and it backfired on her. Rather than sculpering Katrina's chances, Maureen ironically accelerated Simon's non-Soames marital plans. The way it reads, Simon was just happening by the village (during a thunderstorm) and decided to drop in to visit Katrina after supper. It was then that Maureen's audacious Blocker behavior was revealed simultaneously to them both. He immediately invites Katrina to stay at his parents', an ancestral home three hours away, packs her and cat Betsy up, and then phones his mother to fix up the guest room. The next morning, on a hill with a romantic John Constable view, Simon proposes.

Once the engagement of Katrina and the ecstatic Simon made the papers, Maureen really could not show her face in the village. Or in the hospital. Unlike Betty Neels heroines who consider fleeing to Canada or New Zealand, Maureen quickly decamped to a face-saving project in India.

If the Physical Attraction Test does not work on one man, remember there are other fish in the sea. So keep casting. It's a numbers' game.

.

2. Help Him act on his attraction

Ladies, once you have passed his Physical Attraction Test, and he has passed yours, do not think for a second that you can hand off the rest of it to him.

Unless, of course, he is a grownup Gentleman who has internalized The System. In that case, you lucky girl, the Gentleman will act on it by transforming into action. Action Man is going to ask you for your phone number in the brief conversation you two share. In Betty Neels world, Justin Teylingen (*Wish with the Candles*) memorized Emma Hastings' vital information in the 30 seconds he had glanced at her luggage tags.

The System takes into account how busy life is these days. Action Man has a lot on his plate – plus your phone number - and will call you for a date, sooner or later. If he calls to schedule a date a 5 – 9 days after you meet, that's life. Nothing personal so don't take it as a slight.

It is courteous to plan ahead on a date – and the Gentleman will most likely have a coffee date in mind. Betty Neels men do not 'hang out' or go on 'group dates' – later, he invites her to supper or the theatre or dancing. No going to see a movie - on a date with a RDD and a Gentleman, there is conversation involved!

Unfortunately, in real life, so many men these days need a bit of a hand to get going. Even the occasional hero in a Betty Neels book had got to be set straight on how to act on their attraction. Why? Because no one likes to risk the chance of rejection, many men will keep waiting and waiting for a sign you are not going to turn him down. The winner for Best Actor in the role of Inaction Man is a tie between Hugo Van Elven (waited <u>3</u> years in *Fate is Remarkable*) and Dr James Thackery (also 3 years in *Once For All Time*)

You might as well cut to the chase. How? – Ladies can let him know he passes your Physical Attraction test too. Nothing wrong with pointing him in the right direction by signaling your degree of Interest Level (IL), give him a 'buying signal'. Like grade school, if your Interest Level in him is below 50%, he has no chance. By signaling your Interest Level is above 50%, he passes!

So that you can be really clear, you can lightheartedly say, "If you ever want to go out, ask for my phone number. Then call me once you made arrangements."

That makes it clear if he asks you out, rejection is not in the cards. Men tend to dodge rejection, so you are doing him a favour by taking uncertainty out of the picture.

Give him a Cheshire Cat smile and then exit the scene quickly. He can take it as a witty joke or a serious 'buying signal' of Interest Level on your part. Now it is up to him to act on it.

3. First Date /Coffee Date

In order to have a chance at HEA, ladies, you simply start with a mutual Physical Attraction and he follows up with Action with asking you out on a Date, and during the Date, he should show himself a Gentleman. A Gentleman is likely to go the distance. Any sign he is not a Gentleman (Red Flags) and you know the four-letter word is: Next!

As savvy women, we always make sure to have a credit card and cash to get back home in case he turns out to be a cad instead of someone you can bring home to your Mom (poor 27 year old nurse Alethea Thomas in the opening pages of *Sun & Candlelight* when Dr Rat flees the restaurant, sticking her with the bill...)

Keep it light, Keep it funny, No put downs, no heavy subjects
For a successful First Date, Doc Love tells men, is to keep it light, keep it funny, no put downs, no heavy subjects. For some strange reason, English-speaking men like to use sarcasm and put downs. in a weird version of humour – not good at all. A glaringly rude example of put downs is comparing with prettier women - Sybren extolling the beauty of her friend to Rose Comely in *A Girl Named Rose*. And no talking about other dates on your current date – again, here is Sybren in *A Girl Named* Rose taking a call from Mies van Toule during his date with Rose Comely. In the 90 minute maximum coffee date, be respectful and show the lady a good time.

Ladies, it is easy to do likewise. A good time can be had by all if you do not bring up exes. Do not be a bottomless pit of negativity – if you are insecure, geeeez, stop whining about it to all and sundry. It gets tired. Bridget Jones is a fictional character. Don't bring her to life. Instead, act on any drawbacks or flaws in private.

In the novels of Betty Neels, the majority of heroines in the looks department are ordinary women, often described as 'plain' - sometimes readers want to hurl the book across the room when the heroine sobs for the 10th time about her 'lack of looks'. Often she is 'plump' with a bosom. Since when are bosoms beyond the pale?

Either fix it or cope with it. In any event, Get Over It.

And if you are going to fix it, for heaven's sake, blend, ladies, blend! One Blocker, Dr Mary Evans, made changes to her bust size which everyone with eyes can notice took the form of a padded bra (*Once for All Time*).

Check out the Attitude (and the Aptitude)

Doc Love calls the First Date one in which to look at the Attitude and get a sense of what you are each about. You may remember the ending of the pilot episode of the series, Sex & The City. Carrie Bradshaw asked Mr Big, "Have you ever been in love?"

Was his answer to "Have you ever been in love?" fit for mixed company. (Do Google "Sex & The City pilot episode" for the transcript and scroll right to the end.)

Can you imagine a RDD using that kind of language?

That is classic 'testing the waters' – if you accept that kind of behavior on the first date, there's plenty more of that coming your way. That is a Red Flag, don't minimize it, don't explain it, don't ignore it – just say Next!

Betty Neels heroines are so focused on Attitude, they do not go to Brighton on the First Date. (Brighton is euphemism for pre-marital relations). Carrie Bradshaw and Mr Big went straight to Brighton on their first date… and that set the tone for their relationship for the next five years.

Are you each able to take care of yourself and carry your own weight? This is <u>Aptitude</u>. Women have the instinct and disposition to Tend-and-Befriend and support but we are also wise enough to prefer those with the strength to stand on their own two feet. Everyone gets knocked off their feet on occasion and we are there for them. But a man who does not have it in him to be independent is not HEA material. This is where compatibility, companionability, and being classy gets seen.

If these are present and appealing, and you both want to continue to see each other to learn more, then a next date is the logical step!

If mature Attitude and Aptitude are not present, and if you see Red Flags, then The System says one must look at the <u>Bottom Line</u>. The <u>Bottom Line Factor</u> states that Actions are Reality. That's right, what he or she does – not what he or she says – is the truth.

As Doc Love says, Believe it now.

Silicon Valley has a phrase for getting past failure like, Fail fast and fail often. Once you can see this ain't goin' anywhere, then put it behind you ASAP and keep going. Do not let failure immobilize you. Don't mourn your version of Tony the rat (*Daughter of the Manor*). And for heaven's sake, don't develop trust issues of the other gender just because one underdeveloped homo sapiens.

When you believe reality once it presents itself on the coffee date, you do so knowing there are plenty of fish in the sea. It's a numbers game, so Next!

4. Numbers Game

Doc Love spent years in sales so he uses numbers a lot in The System. We women tend to make less use of numbers by focusing on just the number "1". As in, "I think he may be The One." That informs the common notion of dating one fellow exclusively for a stretch of time to decide if he is The One - and then starting over if the answer is no.

The way Doc Love explains it, that's not how it works. Instead, date as many people as possible until you narrow it down. That use of your time seems to me more aligned to what we women do naturally - to approach dating like shopping.

Let's say you are going to a 2-week all-inclusive resort and your checked bag didn't make it on the same flight. The airline gives you a most generous sum of cash in compensation. Time to replenish! Like a Betty Neels heroine, you would get a little of everything – and have fun doing so! That is how you should approach dating.

Not a search for The One but a little of everything – and have fun doing so is a more efficient way of getting to HEA. In *The Course of True Love*, Claribel Brown has an active social life in her off-hours from her physiotherapy job. There are friends aplenty and lots of young men who ask her out – she juggles going out with many men but is exclusive to none. She may be serious but she doesn't take men or dating too seriously.

Being, as she puts it, 'not modern' (when it comes to Brighton), she has her standards and sticks to them. Anyone who has a problem with that can go elsewhere – she does not take it personally.

Taking men too seriously happens in Betty Neels often, making Claribel's sensible approach of dating widely too rare. Examples of dating only one person and then taking a man's rejection to heart and blowing it way out of proportion is Alethea (the ratty Dr Nick) in *Sun & Candlelight*, Sophy Blount *(The Awakened Heart)* and Tishy (and the creep Dr Mike) in *A Small Slice of Summer*. If a man can't take rejection, and starts to get snippy, take it as he is a little boy of 3 who did not get things his way. Do not let his toddler tantrum rip your self-esteem to shreds.

What if your life situation limits the scope of men you meet? Think of Louise Payne in *No Need to Say Goodbye*, whose job was Sister in charge of the Accident department at St Nicholas hospital. You would think living in London would allow her to meet lots of men – ha! She works the night shift. Rachel Downing also worked in a London hospital, in charge of the operating room, but was basically on call 24/7 for emergencies. In chapter 4 of *Off With the Old Love*, she is called at 2 AM to open up the operating room due to an influx of casualties from a riot. Only at 8 PM does Rachel get off work.

These two heroines did not have much waking hours for a social life... almost take what you can get, which is why Rachel put with the swarmy Melville Grant, a TV producer. It is not easy to say, "Next!", when there is no one else on your radar screen.

Nothing makes a woman more vulnerable to putting up with an idiot boyfriend than thinking this is the best she can do.

The solution is to change it up so you can get more of a social life. If it means moving out of living with your whining mom (*Hannah*), going away on vacation instead of staying home to save money (*Caroline's Waterloo*), volunteering (*Two Weeks to Remember*), joining clubs, and finding another job (Phyllida in *Last April Fair*), then do so.

Anything you can do to run up the numbers is a good thing.

5. More Numbers: No Titles til Twelve

Another important number is 12. As Doc Love says, don't take anyone seriously until you have had about 12 dates over three months, no more than once a week. You don't know anybody well enough. The truth about a person, any Red Flags (warning signs), take time to show itself, Bottom Line. The truth about your being able to go the distance as a couple requires Mutual Maturity (MM). Love at first sight certainly happens but sustainable HEA is the goal.

And the title of 'boyfriend' only applies if she asks to be the girlfriend.

I have to give it up to DocLove that his insight that it is the woman who determines the pace and the status of the relationship. After three months or so of no Red Flags (more on that later), it is fair for the lady to talk to him about where this is going.

Let him know she is 'sweet on him' and interested in exclusivity (making sure there are no exes lurking in the background – cut off all contact) and if he is interested in becoming her 'steady'. (An old-fashioned term like 'beau' is also classy.)

Exclusive means no dating other people (or appearing to date Other Woman OW or Other Man OM like Book 34 *Grasp a Nettle*'s Professor Eduard van Draak te Solendijk), no exes lurking in the background (Freule Keizer in *Sister Peters in Amsterdam*) taking down the online dating profile, and not communicating with any exes on FaceBook.

Until you both want to be mutually exclusive, keep up your active dating and social life. In other words, Next!

6. Unnecessary Numbers: Geographic Mileage (AKA no long distance relationships)

To get to HEA, you have to reside close enough to each other to get to know each other. DocLove says distance is a Blocker to getting to know your date over 3 months. If you are more than 90 minutes away from each other, the odds are against you. I agree: Attitude and Aptitude lose out to Geography because you two do not have easy Access to each other on a regular basis.

Long distance does not go the distance because sooner or later, someone has to move. And if that is not going to happen, inevitably you two have to split up. Now, knowing that, why go into something heart-wrenching?

So don't waste your time when distance is a factor. Tough but true.

In *The Awakened Heart*, when Professor Rijk van Taak ter Wijsma tries to persuade Ward Sister Sophie Blount that they could be friends near the end of chapter 1, her reply is "What's the point?" As his home is in the Netherlands and hers is in England, she already sees long distance as a problem and a relationship would be a non-starter. Clever girl!

Ah, but in the romantic novels of Betty Neels, the RDD/RBD has the ways and means to shrink distance!

Jules, the RDD hero in *Discovering Daisy,* secures Daisy, 26, a summer work placement at Heer Fiske's antique shop in Amsterdam. He gets to know her in his hometown to see how intelligent she is – learning Dutch by herself and training with Heer Friske.

Heiress and nurse Esmeralda Jones, 26, in *Esmeralda,* has to travel to the Netherlands for a complex operation on her foot by RDD Thimo Bamstra, 38. The recuperation takes months, during which he is a frequent visitor who shows her the sights of Friesland and Holland and introduces her to his friends and family.

The System's Gentleman and the Lady get to know each other because they have more than 50% Interest Level in each other. The Dating Dictionary depicts the Truth Triangle of what a couple needs as the foundation of a HEA.

It is a bit of a paradox. The Lady wants a Gentleman who is independent, a male strength quality of Aptitude coupled with positive Attitude. She does not want to marry a project, but a fully-mature man. Some men (boys, really) can't cope with life as they lack the 3 essentials of the Gentleman: Confidence, Self-Control, and Challenge. Those boys don't want a partner on the same level (which actually would be a bit of a disastrous couple) but a woman to dominate him as his second mother or a girl to dominate (like social climber Tom who settled for Mies in *Wedding Bells for Beatrice*).

The Gentleman, similarly, is looking for a woman who can take care of herself. Rescuing a woman whose DNA is hardwired for helplessness may appeal to some men, but the Gentleman cannot be bothered to take on that lifelong project. For a HEA, he is looking for Integrity (loyalty being key), Giving (kindness), and Flexibility (responsive to the fluctuations of life).

In the novels of Betty Neels, the heroines on the whole are solid and focused on the here-and-now. An afternoon spent over cups of tea talking about reality, not reality shows, she is the ideal chum. While others may idolize pop stars and fashion trends, her attention is on rescuing animals, serving in church or social committees, and assisting the young and elderly. Nor does she make lifestyle decisions that carry no benefit.

And you can only find that out by proximity.

7. 'Waiting for an Engraved Invitation' Hall of Fame: Men Who Waste Time by Not Asking Her Out

Life's complications make the PA + MM = HEA (Physical Attraction + Mutual Maturity = Happily Ever After) more rare than it should be. Men who like you ask you out. If he does not ask you out, how would a lady ever know he is interested? Doc Love has told too many men to stop being passive! The Wimpus Americanus who doesn't know to ask a woman out (or Inaction Man is too used to things happening on his schedule that he nearly misses his chance at HEA) waste everyone's time. Here are some examples from Betty Neels.

Book 6: *Fate is Remarkable*
After dating for 3 years, London nurse Sarah Dunn, ward sister, 28, gets dumped by Dr Steven for an heiress. Dr Hugo van Elven, 40, proposes a marriage of convenience. Bud, if you had asked her out on a date 4 years ago before Dr Steven even came on the scene, Hugo, there would have been a real marriage 3 years ago right from "I do".

Book 63: *Once For All Time*
Dr James Thackery, 35, has been in love with Clotilde Collins, 25, English nurse (ward sister), since he first laid eyes on her three years ago. Did not ask her out? No, but Dr Bruce did. Bruce and Clotilde have been engaged for almost 2 years when the book opens. Bruce takes off to Leeds after Clotilde's parents die, leaving her with less money than the future son-in-law expected and he takes up with a supermarket heiress. James got her on the rebound.

Did he get (bad) dating tips from Hugo Van Elven?

Book 75: *Off With the Old Love*
Surgeon Radmer van Teule, 35, had known operating room nurse Rachel Downing, 25, for about 2 years before he made a move.

Book 96: *The Quiet Professor*

Professor Baron Jake van Belfeld, 35, waited about 6 months… he at least had an excuse – Megan, 28, had been engaged when they met.

There is acting on it effectively and then there is acting on it with minimal chance of success. Too often, men get the idea from the prevailing culture and media that spontaneous last-minute dates are the way to go. When every woman changes her plans at the drop of a hat when he comes around for a date with no notice (the infamous booty call), an eligible man can get lazy about planning ahead. He thus gets used to not exerting himself – failing to arrange dates ahead of time.

But that is a bad habit that can work against him. Betty Neels illustrated what can happen when a man takes a woman's acceptance for granted: Professor Ross Dieperink van Berhuys in Book 33. *A Gem of a Girl* found out that hard way that not every women will immediately clear her schedule for him. The Professor, 37, simply drove by to take her out to dinner – only to find that the putz Leo Voss had beaten him to Gemma Prentice, 24, and had gotten a date commitment from her already. Gemma, being a lady, was not going to jilt her date in favour of Ross, who fumed as they drove away.

Ross learnt his lesson and basically stalked Leo and Gemma on each of their subsequent dates. In *The System*, a Gentleman does not trashtalk the competition; he simply shows up the other guy. (Leo takes Gemma to a half-basement restaurant whereas Ross wines and dines her in style. Knowing Leo could be playing her false, now-Action Man Ross kept an eye on her, ready to pick up the pieces as it were. With confidence.

Organizing ahead of time beats the element-of-surprise offer each and every time.

8. Red Flags

When you get to know someone, their Red Flags slowly reveal themselves. Some are not important to you; some are critical and turn out to be Deal Breakers.

a. If she hates your dog and cat, then that is the Red Flag. Professor Christian van Duyl's fiancée, beanpole Estelle, was not an animal person in Book 29 *Heaven is Gentle*. And Helena Thornfeld actually kicked his dog, Bellow, in *An Ideal Wife...* in front of him!

b. If you can't agree on religion, then that is a Red Flag. In Betty Neels, the heroines were inevitably COE (Church of England or Scotland, definitely Protestant), same as the RBD (unless he was Scottish) while the RDD were Calvinists.

c. If money is a problem now, it's going to be a big problem later. None of the heroes or heroines have money problems caused by drink or drugs or careless spending. Several heroines have to deal with parents oblivious to money but she herself is good at cheeseparing (The Hastings women raise hens, sell eggs, and share the car in *Wish with the Candles*.)

d. Does he prefer fantasies to reality? If he fancies video gaming a couple hours a day now, it is going to dominate your marriage later = Deal Breaker. Or is his fantasy that his upper crust fiancée would undergo a metamorphosis from bony & haughty to warm & wonderful? That should a Deal Breaker (one is curious how Betty Neels heroes could be so blind to that – or maybe too arrogant to see it. We (I am speaking for Louisa Payne too) are looking at you, Dr Thomas Gifford, *An Ideal Wife*.

If the parents do not like your fiancé(e), that is a Red Flag. Book 27, *The Moon for Lavinia*, Professor Radmer ter Bavinck's mother did not care at all for his first wife. In Book 70 Never The Time and the

Place, mama's boy Malcolm's mother does not get along with heroine, Josephine Dowling. She wises up and dumps him.

Besides the above five, I go into a bit more detail about four more Red Flags.

When you see them, decide if they are going to drive you nuts. In short, if you have everything in common but a harmonious future, then call it a day now.

e. <u>Earn Your Keep?</u>

It is nice when a man offers to help you carry your bags. It is very nice if he is a RDD! Like attracts like – it is not the action but the ability to do the action. Most RDD/RBD in the Canon want to show chivalry, but they don't want to be the donkey to a woman who is helpless and hopeless. Veronica (short form for Her Rival for His Affections) has the means to make sure their bags are carried.

Ladies, you need to get skills when you can.

Daisy Gillard, Book 124 *Discovering Daisy*, is the most entrepreneurial heroine in the entire Canon – and earmarked to take over the family business, her father's respected antique shop. She has an eye out for quality antiques, has experience purchasing and negotiating price, restoring, and is intelligent enough to train. She does research. She knows her stuff. She likes her calling.

Like other heroines of Betty Neels, Daisy has her high school credentials - 2 A levels - and could have gone on to university but in Daisy's case, it makes sense that she focus on the shop and on-the-job training Antiques are in her blood – she could host Antiques Road Show.

Henrietta Cowper (Book 113 *Only By Chance*), an orphan who had no chance to train for a career, had a legitimate reason for her lack of marketable skills. Sad to say, quite a few other Betty Neels heroines do not. They had their heads in the sand regarding getting a job. Really, who does that in this day and age? More than you would think!

These ladies are unskilled either by circumstance or oblivious 'ninnyhead' hiding their heads in the sand about getting employment skills.

Here is 24 year old Cressida (Book 95. *A Happy Meeting*) whose father recently died, and left everything to the stepmother, with the understanding that his daughter was to be provided for. Waiting to see if stepmother would change her stripes… not a good strategy, Cressy.

Book 86. *A Suitable Match.* Eustacia Crump, 22, reached the age of 20 when her wealthy parents died. Product of a private school education, she had travelled the world with her family, postponing higher education in a multi-year Gap Year. When they died, she had no marketable skills. The Gap Year is a First-World Problem.

Book 88. *Roses Have Thorns.* Sarah Fletcher, 28, has been on her own for 5 years. Her mother died when Sarah was a teen, and her father then remarried a witch. Wouldn't that be a clue to take up career training? For some reason, Sarah did not. When Dad Fletcher died, she was 23 and had to take a course in secretarial skills because stepmother turned her out of the family home.

Book 106. A Christmas Wish. Olivia Harding is 27, her father died leaving them penniless when she was 23. So what was she doing from age 17 when she finished high school to age 23? Plenty of time to get serious about marketable skills!

The final Betty Neels, Book 135 *Emma's Wedding*, featured 27-year old Emma who stays at home living off the fat of the land. Until her father dies and there is only thing left is a cottage at seaside Salcombe.

An RDD doesn't come along every day – and when that happens, she got to be at least trying to get by. Emma Dawson, having moved her mother and herself to Salcombe turns a hand at housecleaning, reception, library – and earns the respect of Dr Roele van Dyke for her Attitude and her belated Aptitude.

So keep up with the times and keep current so you will always be able to earn your keep.

f.   Talks About Exes?

A HEA is the future. An ex is history. History that is dead and buried. Leave it up to the archeologists to dig up fossilized history, don't you bring it up. That applies to both Ladies and Gentlemen. Examples of learning this the hard way in the Betty Neels canon are below…

Book 90. *The Final Touch*
Mevrouw de Groot is his ex and Dr Cor van Kemp is hers. Tyco van der Brons, 40, as influential as he is in Amsterdam, can't get Cor fired so if moving the entire household to Friesland in Book 95 *A Happy Meeting* is the only way to never cross paths with his 23 year old wife's ex, then that's what you.

Book 2. *A Match for Sister Maggy*
Paul van Beijnen Doelsma, tsk tsk tsk… Telling the woman you intend to propose to that you have wined and dined many previous dates at that same divine restaurant will get you publicly dumped at Schipol Airport. Mr Smarty Pants, you better pack the big guns of family jewels and Special Licence cause that's the only way to prove to nurse Maggy McPherson that you have marriage on your mind.

Book 6. *Fate is Remarkable*
Hugo, you dolt… next time ex-flame, Janet, or any ex-girlfriend has marital problems, and you want to help, do not secretly meet her at Fortnum & Mason, hold her hand, and get spotted by your wife.

In fact, save your breath and time and energy and help and give your ex the number for the nearest MFT.

Or you will be the one with marital problems. And trotting 6 miles through Scottish snowdrifts carrying tinned milk.

Book 8. *Tangled Autumn*
Same goes for the ladies, never talk about your ex and never talk to your ex.

Do let everyone know he is your ex – and that it is done and buried. Otherwise, Bold and Bad Baron will jump to conclusions (and everyone else in the book too) and leap over a HEA.

g. To Tell The Truth

If things do not add up, that is a Red Flag.

Nurse Serena Potts was dating Dr Laurens van Amstel (Book 13. *Uncertain Summer*) whom everyone on his side of the family knew was getting engaged to Adriana. Even the hero, Gijs, lies to Serena, claiming Adriana was his own girlfriend. No one tells Serena this truth, until Lauren's sour-faced mother decided to spill the beans. It is a kindness to disclose this sort of vital information ASAP, people!

Melville Grant was a 'busy' TV producer whose colleague Pat Morris outted his skimpy work schedule to nurse Rachel Downing in *Off with the Old Love*.

Fortune hunting cousin Mervyn in Book 15 *Winter of Change* could never produce a bill and got defensive when confronted by heroine nurse Mary Jane. If vague replies or moodiness is the response to a call for the truth, you already have your answer.

Fairly innocuous play on the truth, wealthy baron and professor of medicine Jeroen van der Glissen, in *The Little Dragon*, vainly trying to keep up the appearance of being an ordinary family doctor in front of his new bride, the obvious nurse Constantia Morley.

One of the lowest things a man can do is to trot out some woman to provoke jealousy. Deception is not gentlemanly – it uses two women, raises the hopes of one and the ire of the other. This pathetic tacitc is sprinkled throughout the Betty Neels canon, including Professor Renier Jurres-Romeijn using beautiful Heleen to make nurse Emily Seymour, 23, jealous (Book 46 *Winter Wedding*).

h. Organized or Sloppy & Disorganized?

It is not easy to track down examples in the Betty Neels canon of RDD/RBD being disorganized. But for you, I go the extra mile:

Book 81. The Fateful Bargain – Professor Jonkheer Sebastian van Tecqx did not organize Emily Grenfell's off-hours from caring for his extremely spoiled sister or telling her about the security system in his mansion in Delft. Although he did a magnificent job making sure her father's operations and recuperation went flawlessly, on each hip.

Haso van der Eisler failed to pay Olivia Harding, a very cash-strapped Olivia, in Book 106 *A Christmas Wish*.

Widower/surgeon Dominic van Wijkelen, 40, forgets to pay nurse Abigail, 24, twice, in *Saturday's Child*, Book 12. His first wife left him only half a year after they got married – and he has been a walking bitter man ever since (that's another Red Flag).

The sloppiest hero has got to be Professor Radolf Nauta in Book 88 *Roses Have Thorns*. He swears Sarah Fletcher to secrecy, a promise that gets her fired from her job at the hospital. Without many options, she takes her cat, Charles, and sets off to the nearest issue of The Lady to find work as a maid.

9. The Naturals: The 3% of Gentlemen

There you have it – Physical Attraction + mutual maturity = HEA (shortened to PA + MM + HEA.) Gentlemen who have it together when it comes to dating show up in Betty Neels. He sees the means to his HEA and acts on it. Because he knows women. He is a rarity who is born understanding women, a Natural, only 3% of the male population.

Walle van der Tacx, *Philomena's Miracle*

Dr Walle van der Tacx, 36, is waiting for the elevator in the hospital where Philly, 23, just named Gold Medalist of her year in nursing, is transporting a patient. Acting fast, that very night, Walle asks her out, to 'celebrate' her achievement as a new state registered nurse. The following night when the patient dies, the doctor comforts her with late night fish & chips. A weekend later, Walle just happens to drive down to the small town near her country home. Having had enough of the long-distance dating, Walle gets rid of the Blocker known as geography by arranging a nursing job for her in The Netherlands.

Simon Glenville, *The Innocent Bride*

The moment he meets Katrina Gibbs, 24, whose bicycle was sideswiped along the country road, Professor Simon Glenville, 39, rearranges his schedule to see more of her. He cannot get her out of his mind so he rearranges his schedule to see more of her. They have many interests in common: Her cottage has a garden – his home has a garden. They both love madrigals. They get along. She's a keeper - so Simon proposes and they have a white wedding.

Gideon van der Vorst, *The Magic of Living*

Awesome in saving the cerebral palsy children on the bus – 23 year old Arabella Birch's creativity in making use of his swimming pool for Billy and Sally's recuperation earns his admiration - and Gideon, 38, follows her back to London intent on marriage.

You can say that they all got game – and a game plan.

ABOUT THE AUTHOR

Janice Seto writes non-fiction and commentary including articles for The Bridge, the publication of The Malaysia-Canada Business Council. Her most recent books are available on Amazon: *Standing Out in The Background – A Guide to Extra Work in Toronto's Film & TV Industry, Segovia Restaurant – Espana in Toronto by Ino, Bowmanville's Octagon House – From Church and Faith and Tait to Irwin & Seto, Johnny's Place - The Coronation Restaurant in Bowmanville*, and *Johnny Seto's Bowmanville – An Enneagram Perspective.*

The System for Women is her first book series on relationships.

Betty Neels is the modern Jane Austen – give it a few more years, and the world will be convinced, not just the ladies of The Uncrushable Jersey Dress blog, http://everyneelsthing.blogspot.com/

Janice gets her laughs via the Doc Love podcast and weekly radio show, accessible to members of the DocLoveClub http://www.doclove.com/ . Newcomers welcome!

www.janiceseto.com
http://janiceseto.wix.com/words

www.ingramcontent.com/pod-product-compliance
Lightning Source LLC
Chambersburg PA
CBHW060644030426
42337CB00018B/3443